A Kid's Guide To Elite Hikes of Sedona

If you are visiting Sedona with your family and are wondering where the most fun your kids can have while Hiking, there is nowhere else you need to look.

This guide book is for the Mom and Dad that wants to BLOW YOUR KID'S MINDS while experiencing Sedona. Whether on a day visit, a weekend, or a long vacation week, we will guide you to the Best of the Best that Sedona has to offer with your kids in mind!

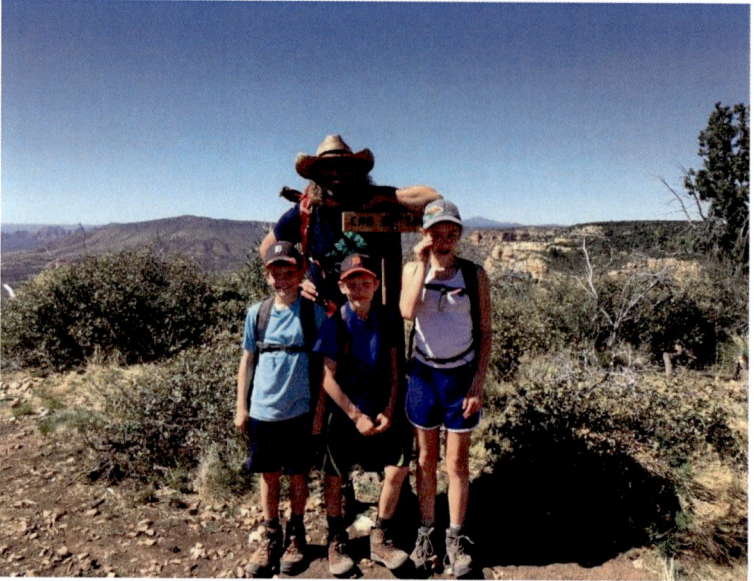

The A Kid's Guide to Elite Hikes of Sedona

Part of the Bearclan's 'Elite Sedona Hikes' Series

By: Soaring Bear

Yava-Coco Publishing

2018

First Printing: 2018

ISBN: 9781791616724

Yava-Coco Publishing
441 Forest Road
Sedona, Arizona 86336

www.yavacocoproductions.com

Dedication

To the spirit of Hiking!

As a fourth-generation hiker having my Great Grandfather as a trail blazer in the Green Mountains of Vermont, this desire was instilled in me as a child as far back as I can remember. My two sons were introduced to it early on in their childhood as well and have taken part in some incredible hiking adventures including spending the night in my Great Grandfather's Shelter along the Long Trail in Vermont with me, my brother and my father making it a 3 generation overnight memory.

*The Hiking Spirit is created when we introduce our children to the magic of exploration. Even if it is a flat trail in a park, when we see their eyes light up as they watch their first Hawk fly, or Rabbit scamper or even when they touch their first flower or tree, we see that special moment of **Feeling** the life that surrounds them.*

Let's celebrate the Hiking Spirit by sharing it with our children.

Contents

Acknowledgments

I would like to thank my two sons; Johnathan and Carter, as they were willing and excited participants to explore and hike with me as they were growing up. Though their passion for hiking isn't quite equal to mine, I hope they someday return to the adventures of the great outdoors. The love I have for them is immeasurable and forever and I am eternally grateful that they have grown up to be Good Men!

PREFACE

SAFETY TIPS

BE SAFE - In the last three years (2015-2017), Sedona has seen an increase in Search and Rescue cases reaching over 1500 per year! I mention this because of the true hard facts about hiking in the desert. The three major things we find are people not drinking enough water and dehydrating, hiking where you don't belong and people thinking soda or alcohol are a good thing to consume before going outside for any activity. The elements out here are very different than many places on earth and the dry air and hot sun does not show you typical signs of losing moisture. It's really simple; if you feel thirsty, you are already suffering from dehydration out here. Drink water especially when you are ***not*** thirsty!

CAUSE NO HARM - Another thing that I need to stress here is that I do what I do with respect and honor of the land. I will not leave anything behind and I try, to the best of my ability, not to damage the land...ever! Us local avid hikers understand that accidents happen and mistakes are made, but do not come here to "Rip-It-Up" unless you are referring to your own body. We are not your mothers or fathers, but we are all stewards of the land and we need to keep Sedona a place to enjoy visiting and experiencing through hiking. If people keep throwing their garbage away in the woods, there is a chance Sedona can be shut down to public access. That is no lie. It has been addressed and is in consideration. So PLEASE keep Sedona clean!

FIRE DANGERS - Open fires in Sedona should be understood as not a good idea. This land is desert and the trees and shrubs here are ridiculously dry and can catch fire easily enough with a tiny spark from an open fire or a dropped cigarette butt. I use a small, compact fuel burner kit, that when tipped, it shuts off automatically. That is the only way to cook or heat something up without possibly causing a forest fire. We have one or two fires each year caused by people not watching or not fully putting out their fires. A small gust of wind is enough to set things off and there are days that the gusts can reach 30-40mph or higher. PLEASE be cautious and never leave a fire unattended!

LEASH LAWS - Sedona actually has a Leash Law for dogs on trails. Just this morning I was on a hike with a friend and two pet owners came by us and **both** of them had two dogs and **both** of their dogs were not on a leash. I am a dog lover and I understand the desire to do this to allow your wonderful pet the freedom to roam, but because other locals are not so keen on animals, they may not react like I did. Some of those folks may also have weapons to protect themselves and if your dog shows signs of unease, something very bad could happen and it would be your fault for not leashing it. It's an ugly topic of discussion, but it *is the law*!

STATISTICS - used in this Guide Book are based on my use of technology (GPS), multiple map references and other research I've done over the last 10 years. One map's information may not be the same as another, so things such as elevations, elevation gains, degree of grade and so on will most likely be different everywhere you look. An example would be a staggering difference in the summit elevation of Wilson Mountain; Beartooth Publishing shows 7045ft, Emmitt Barks Cartography shows 7122ft and my Altimeter App shows 7118ft. So keep that in mind and use the numbers as a "guide" to your journey!

INTRODUCTION

Sedona, Arizona. The home of the Red Rocks. Also known as the Day Hike Capitol of the United States! With over 150 trails to choose from (and growing), Sedona has an immeasurable count of destinations and challenges for your entire family. You bought this book, so that means you are extremely interested in bringing your children to the most enjoyable hikes Sedona has to offer.

"A Kid's Guide to Elite Hikes of Sedona" is exactly what it claims, brining you and your kids to the best possible places for a Family to touch and feel the Red Rocks in the safest way possible with incredible views.

Make this family journey the most memorable *ever* as your young hikers explore trails, rocks, boulders, climbing, un-ending views, and photographic moments that their friends (and yours) will be completely envious of. You are on your way to becoming an ELITE Hiker of Sedona's Red Rocks!

In this guide book, I will introduce you to the perfect ELITE Kid's Trails, their locations, their equipment required (if any) and the details from bottom to the top (and sometimes back). This is simply just THE BEST Kids Hikes Sedona has to offer.

Elite Kid's Hike number 1:

Name: Bell Rock

Defined: Shaped like a "Bell", this 600ft+ rock formation is a veritable playground for your kids (even the older ones!). It is the hike I tell ALL the families to explore. It provides wide open areas to run, play, climb, test skills, and the views are over the top!

A Red Rock Parking Pass is required to hike here and for most of Sedona's hiking trails. Assume you need it when hiking any of these trails listed unless otherwise noted.

Trail Details: There are two access points to Bell; **Bell Rock Vista Parking Lot** and **Courthouse Butte Vista Parking Lot**. Both are located on Rte. 179 near the Village of Oak Creek. The easiest access is from Courthouse Butte Vista Parking Lot as Bell Rock is a mere .3 miles from your parked vehicle. Bell Rock Vista Parking Lot is roughly 1.3 miles from Bell Rock but the photographic opportunities of Bell Rock are far more impressive from this entrance. Let's review them both.

Bell Rock Vista Access: Take Route 179 N or S until you see the signage on the road for the Bell Rock Vista Parking Lot. It is located 6.2 miles from the ""Y"" round-about in Uptown Sedona and 8.2 miles from Highway 17.

As you come in to the parking lot, you will notice a small shack-looking building on the right side only a hundred feet or so from the entrance. This shack is a great kiosk

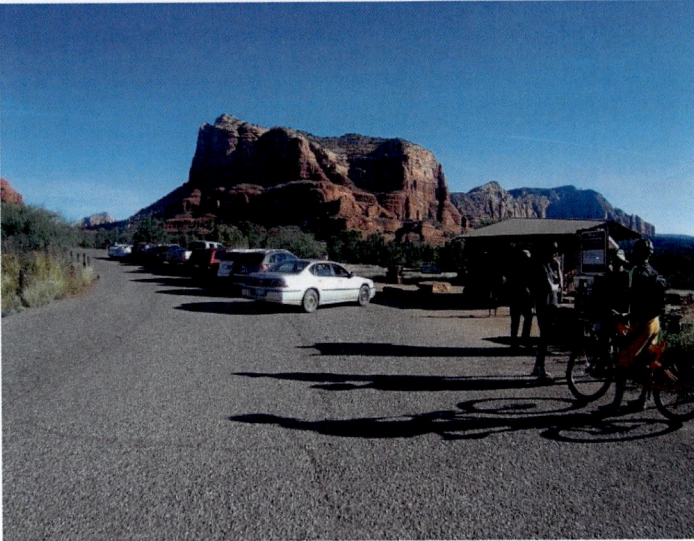

filled with information about Bell Rock and Courthouse Butte and acts as a small shaded spot to recover from a long day of playing. On the right side of that shack is where the trail begins. Park your car and walk to the shack to start your adventure.

The short pathway is fenced and will start eastward towards the flat mesas and the eastern section of the Village of Oak Creek. You will then turn northward and immediately get to see why they call it Bell Rock as the entire structure is shaped similarly to a bell.

The trail is approximately 1 mile long and the views are magnificent along the way. It is a very well maintained trail with nicely marked signage. As you get closer to Bell, your photographic moments will be limitless and your desire to get there and start climbing will be even more exciting than your first viewing of her majestic construction.

The trail will split at around .6 miles in where you could hike the Courthouse Butte Loop Trail, but stay to your **left** as it brings you in a westerly direction hugging the base of Bell. There are ample spots for pictures so enjoy!

Soon, you will be cruising upwards on a very slight slope easily maneuvered by anyone and there will be some fun rocks on the ground for the younger kids to enjoy. The trail will travel between Bell Rock and Route 179 (see image below) and the main access point to begin your Bell Rock experience will be to the North end (at the right of the yellow oval on the image below) as you continue on the trail.

I highly recommend taking the extra .5 mile walk to the North end of Bell and follow the "Trail" signs to enter your wide open Red Rock playground. It will act as a testing grounds for you and your family. This way you can see how well, and more importantly, how safely your kids manage the Red Rocks.

There will be clear signage as you progress around Bell Rock, so as long as you stay on the main trail, you will always know where you are and where you are heading.

Once you arrive at the North end, it will look less like a Bell and more like a wide-open area of enjoyment.

At the North end of Bell, you can take any of the options heading onto the rock. Some of these access points

will bring you some quick hand and feet scampering; sort of an introduction to finding out how good your traction is and your abilities to use your hands and feet as you climb/boulder your way around. You can see the potential from the previous image.

If you prefer the quicker access up, then fade into Bell before you get to the signage. Essentially, just as you start curling away from the road, there will be mini off-chute trails that will take you up a more easily accessed area. This option could be used for the younger children or the older adults.

When you decide on your entry point, the rest is up to you. Right, left, up, down. It will all be an exciting experience and will create memories for a lifetime!

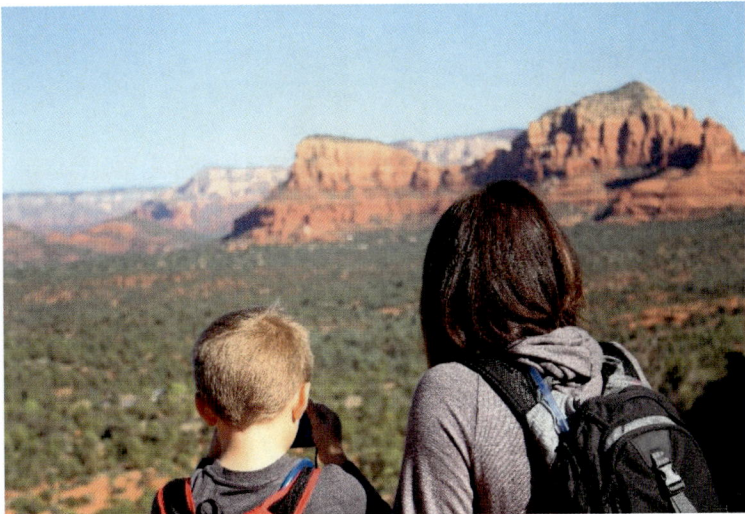

From this area of Bell, you will be able to walk 300 degrees around Bell Rock and explore to your hearts

content. Understand fully, that if you have younger children, it is in your best interest to stay close to them and always make sure they are safe even in the flat areas.

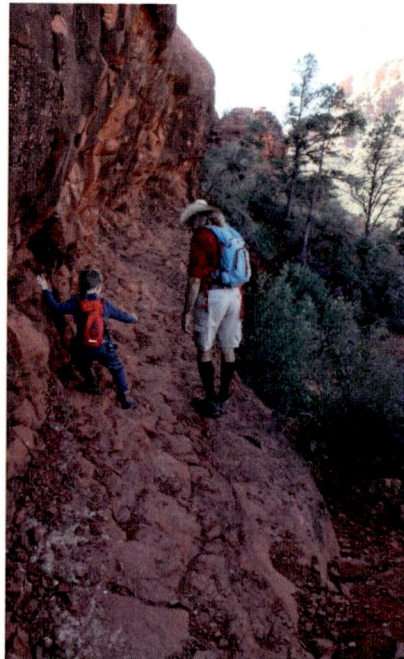

The next option, for the older families, will be to summit certain areas. There are two attractive locations on Bell that are reasonable to attain; North End Perch and the South End Perch. Both require substantial skill and a desire to climb up. Be careful how you do this, because in Sedona; "What goes Up...MUST come down!" If the image below is scary, then keep to the low ground. Otherwise, we will introduce you to the high points of Bell.

Since these directions have brought you to the North end of Bell, it makes sense that we attack the North End Perch first.

The North End Perch is located high above the playground area and is intimidating to many, but perfectly suited for the more skilled or adventurous types.

As you can see from the image above, the access seems pretty simple, and it is. Just follow that seam that is below and to the right of the Perch to complete the easy part. Then, you will find a tight climb behind the Perch that will provide you the summit of the Perch.

You will have to maneuver around a couple of the Juniper trees and then it is hand and feet work wrapping you around, and behind the first Perch and giving you ample access to either of the Perches for stupendous visuals and photographic opportunities as you look into the City of Sedona in a picturesque brilliance.

The second option I call; The South Perch. It is a high spot about half way to the top and on the Southwest face of Bell Rock (closer to Route 179).

This is no easy get as it requires some work in a steep seam that is approximately 100 yards in length. Accessing that seam starts on the West side of Bell, nearest the highway. Since these directions have described the Bell Rock Vista Parking access, we will use that as our access point. Know fully, that either Trail Head will get you to these locations. It all depends on your desires for quicker access, or more photographic access.

We will assume that you've read the directions to accessing Bell Rock from the Bell Rock Vista Parking Lot and we will begin the directions for this Perch from the point shown in the image below. You can see the trails that are near the road. These are the best access points for this Perch (image below is not the perch, just a visual of the trails from above).

Once you find yourself on the Western side of Bell, you will see many small off-chutes that appear to bring you to the layers on your right. Your goal is to find that first trail (shown at the left side of the image below) and head into the flowing rocks. The desired path will take you up to a very large Juniper tree that is the beginning of the Seam work.

*The highlights in the image at left are another view of the access point for this Perch.

You will know you are at the right seam because it will look doable. The seam just before it will not be anything you can climb and if you go too far, you will find that little spire on the right side (see the far right side just after the red arrow in the darker image above), then you will have to back track to the proper seam.

The seam is pretty wide, but there are a few points along the climb that will pinch you in. You will also have to climb a tree (yes...you heard me) but there are many obvious foot placements available to make it easy enough and the trees that are growing here are very well rooted. I use them and I am 6' 2" and about 220lbs, so you can most likely trust the tree. Just don't take anything for granted as a lot of people hike Bell and anyone could potentially harm or cause damage to it and make it an unsafe climb. The image below shows the small tree access.

As mentioned before, this seam is a decent climb. There will be a couple 'escapes' from the climb as you get nearer the top. They will look like great places to jut out and see the views, but stick to the plan, the seam ends at the Perch top. You will know you are almost at the top when you see a few Prickly Pear cacti in the way.

When you arrive at the Perch, you will have this large cap of Red Rocks to play on and you will be able to see almost the entire Village of Oak Creek below you. You may find rock art left behind by travelers, but you will have no shortage of picture moments.

Ideally, you will want to arrive as early as possible as this is one of Sedona's most popular hiking areas and you can meet up with a lot of other adventure seekers as you cruise around the base of Bell. An alternative option is to hike Bell for a gorgeous sunset as you will be able to see the brilliant color changes of the night as you look down into the heart of the City of Sedona and her magnificent Red Rock vistas.

Courthouse Butte Vista Access: In essence, the only thing needing to be said here is that you can get closer to Bell by parking at this lot. It is .2 miles from Bell and brings you to the North side. Other than that, it is very much the same as the Bell Rock Vista entrance once you arrive at the North end of the Bell Rock formation.

At the parking lot, there will be a kiosk similar to the Bell Rock Vista entrance and the fencing next to it clearly shows you the path to Bell Rock. Once you enter the

pathway, there will be clear signage showing you the way to climb Bell Rock. The Bell Rock Pathway is the trail that starts at the Bell Rock Vista Parking Lot, so you don't need to worry about that here as you are now just minutes away from the enormous fun with hiking and playing with Bell Rock!

Trail Head Maps:

Bell Rock:

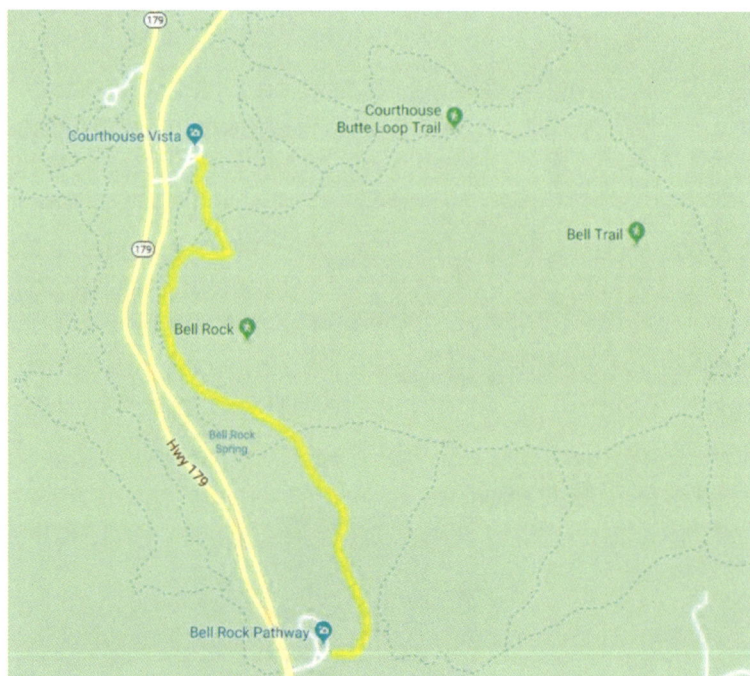

Distance (One Way):

Bell Rock Vista Parking Lot: 1.1 Miles

Courthouse Vista Parking Lot: 0.3 Miles

Elevation Gain: **Approximately 100-300ft**

Equipment Required:

- Something with great traction. Rubber soles work best for Bell. Sneakers with synthetic rubber aren't as good as rubber soles
- Ample water! Anywhere you hike in Sedona requires water. If you think you have enough, get a little more

- Great cameras or really nice cell phone cameras. Pictures here are ridiculous!
- Snacks are ideal because there are gobs and gobs of stopping points for rest, relaxing, meditating and eating

Key Notes:

Bell Rock was my very first hike in Sedona. EVER! I entered Sedona on Route 179 and when I came around the corner, I saw it and I began to cry! Something called me to her and I hiked her within the first 30 minutes of my Sedona experience. I stumbled on the South Perch and it changed my life. I felt this dramatic pull to eventually live in Sedona, and here I am!

The trick to hiking Bell safely is to ensure your traction is exactly what Bell needs; rubbery traction with good flexible soles and do not venture past your comfort zone! There are many Search and Rescues off Bell each year because folks forget the key element to climbing; "What goes up...MUST come down!". If you are questioning your choice, ALWAYS defer to safety first. In the words of Clint Eastwood from Dirty Harry; "A man's gotta know his limits." Please...know your limits and don't push it! We want you to be safe, not a statistic!

Elite Kid's Hike number 2:

Name: Fay Canyon

Defined: Fay Canyon is a short, but sweet hike in the back west side of Sedona away from the residential areas. Quiet and quaint and mostly flat with dry creek beds throughout, it is walled between the Red Rocks with exceptional views and photographic scenes at every corner.

A Red Rock Parking Pass is required to hike here and for most of Sedona's hiking trails. Assume you need it when hiking any of these trails listed unless otherwise noted.

Trail Details: With only one entrance, this trail is easy to find and access, as well as hike. The greatest attributes are that you are enclosed with gorgeous formations throughout the entire hike as you are nestled inside a tight canyon.

The Trail Head parking lot is located on Boynton Pass Road which is exactly 5 miles from the intersection of

89A and Dry Creek Road and located on the left hand side of the road. The trail is across the road from the parking lot and there are two paths to get to the trail, both within 100 feet of each other. You will see the trail sign confirming you are headed in the right direction.

Once you are on the trail, you will sneak through some

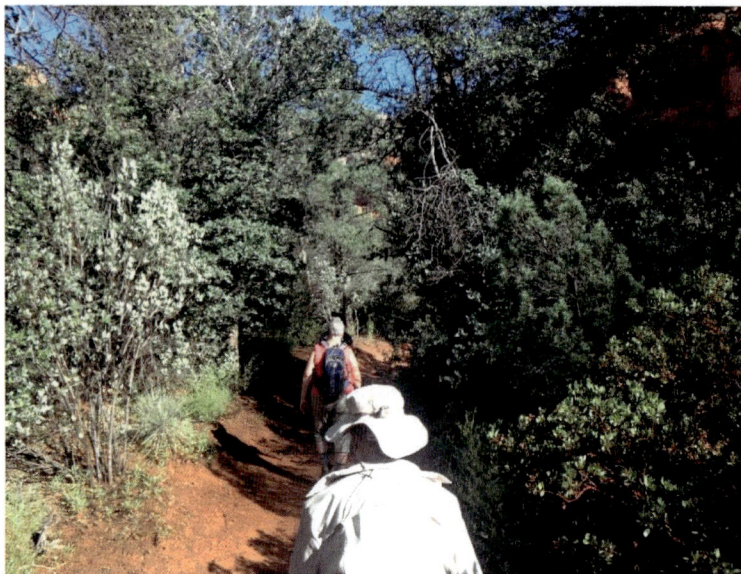

juniper and cypress trees and then you'll be out into the wide open for a few hundred yards or so, You will then be into the canyon for a majority of your hike.

You will cross over a dry creek a few times as you progress onward. The trail is exceptionally marked, so as long as you stay on the trail, you will be in good shape. About .5 miles into your hike, you may be able to see the Fay Canyon Arch (located on your right), but it will take perfect timing to recognize it as it blends into the walls perfectly. If you are on the trail from noon or after, there will be a slight shadow cast on the back side of the Arch providing you with a little clarity. The image below was taken from the same level as the Arch so you can see its placement:

Continuing on your canyon hike, you will see foliage
and colors throughout the year, but depending on when
you arrive and hike, you may see a multitude of floral
colors or the sages growing along the walk.

The benefit of hiking Sedona is that we have a tendency to have colors almost year round as something seems to be blooming each month and season. Mid to late spring is the highest concentration of colors as our cacti tend to be lighting up the landscapes then.

The trail will meander in a mini-switch-back style for the remainder of your hike and you will be blessed with unlimited photo opportunities as you travel.

When you arrive at the end of the trail, you will be notified of it with signage.

If you look at the sign, you will notice it says; "END OF MAINTAINED TRAIL". That means you can turn around and head back, or you can scamper a little further forward to find a playground for your entire family.

The rocks are not stable here so don't assume your footing will be perfect. There are two areas to venture out in from the Eagle's Head tree (image below), into

the low brush at the right, or up into the rocks straight ahead. I prefer to have everyone scoot up the rocks so that they can look back from where they came with incredible photographs.

Trail Head Maps:
Fay Canyon:

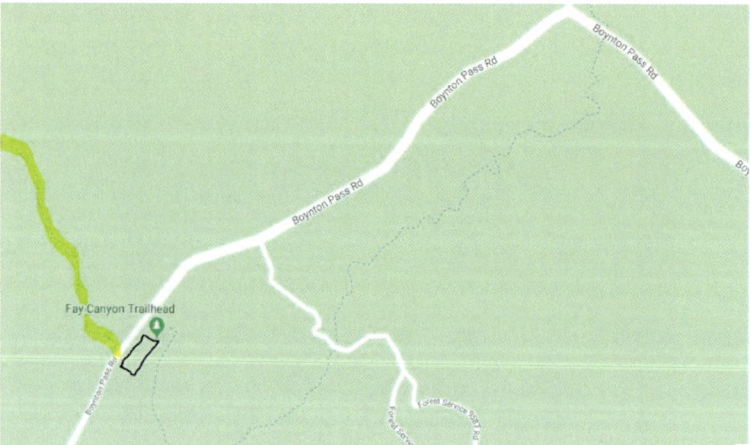

Distance (One Way):

Fay Canyon Parking Lot: 1.3 Miles

Elevation Gain: Approximately 100-300ft

Equipment Required:

- Something real comfortable. Sneakers, sandals, hiker boots are all fine
- For summer months, ensure you have plenty of water. Even though the canyon has tree cover, it is still necessary to have water with you.
- Great cameras or really nice cell phone cameras as usual
- Snacks

Key Notes:

Fay Canyon has been a tried and true hike for just about everyone. Its simplicity, short distance and ease makes it perfect for every family regardless of age. It is not technical until you get to the end and up in the rocks, but there are many places to sit and just soak in the sublime energy that surrounds you. Year round hikes will provide you with perfection in pictures so there will be no shortage of that on any day.

Watch your footings as there are some small tree stumps and roots here and there and you could get tripped up if you aren't careful. Other than that, this walk/hike will be enjoyed by all who follow her path.

Elite Kid's Hike number 3:

Name: West Fork

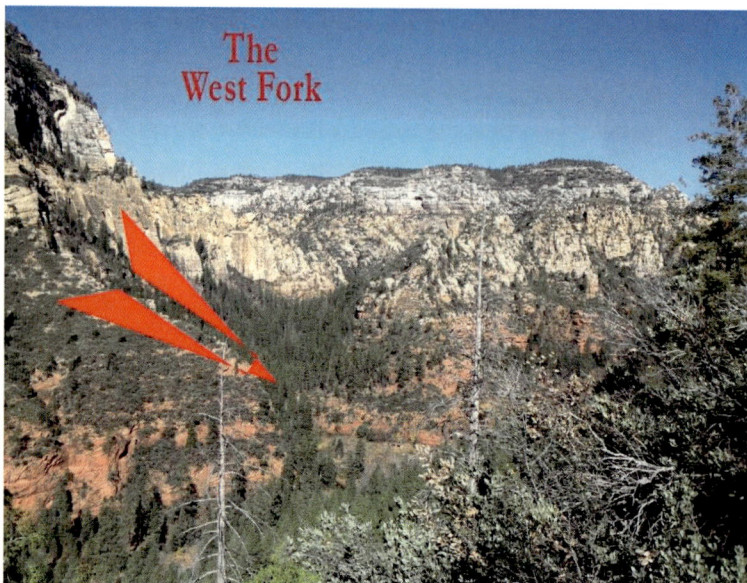

Defined: West Fork is commonly known to the locals as; Call Of The Canyon picnic area, as it is partial home to the old Western movie filmed in Sedona back in 1923 of the same name. Call of the Canyon was a Zane Grey novel turned movie and parts of the movie were filmed in Oak Creek Canyon. The trail itself is approximately 3.3 miles in length and is crossed by the West Fork of Oak Creek 16 times offering up a plethora of stopping points to enjoy the cool waters and relaxing.

*A Red Rock Parking Pass is not applicable here, either a Grand Annual Red Rock Pass or a $10/car Fee will be required. See Entrance Gate personnel for more details.

Trail Details: Located in the northern section of 89A North in Sedona about 10.6 miles from the "Y" round-about in Uptown Sedona, West Fork Trail head can be a hard get especially during spring break, the hot summer months, and holidays as there is limited parking. What I suggest is plan ahead and think about arriving very early (gates open at 9AM) or on off-peak seasons, which truthfully, winter is about the only off-season for West Fork, unless we get snow!

Once you arrive and park your vehicle, you will look for the large rock structure for the beginning of the trail:

The trail pathway starts out as a cement sidewalk (as you can see to the right of the previous image) and you gradually enter the narrow tree-covered section that

carries you to what seems to be a grand entrance into the history of a Sedona settlement with a gentle walk over a metal bridge, a viewing of the remains of the Mayhew Cabin and storage (next page) and a quick sampling of where some of the apple trees grew during our apple orchard days.

All of this is seen before you get to the good stuff!

A windy, easy up and down path begins and you are now in the thick of West Fork's hot spots. Even though the trail is a mere 3.3 miles, the potential for stopping and taking pictures can make this seem like a lot longer, but it is beyond worth the efforts as you will see.

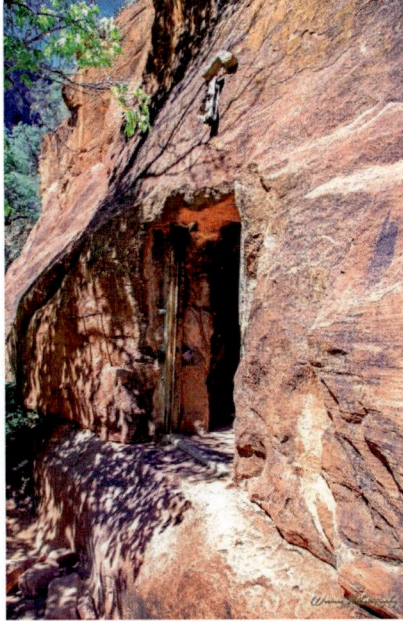

There are some sections of creek crossing that may be hard to distinguish where the trail ends or begins. Keep

it simple and look directly across from where you meet the creek and scan no more than 25 feet either left or right and you should pick up the 'other side' easily enough.

Early views of the creek are spectacular captures of formations that make the mind wonder how these enormous special rocks were created.

As you work your way through the thickets and the incredibly tall Ponderosa Pine forest, you will kiss the side of the creek the entire journey.

There will be ample spots for rest and relaxation and even for deep meditation. Sometimes you won't be able to tell if it is resting or meditating as they may appear to be exactly the same!

Back and forth the path crosses the creek. Slight ups and downs and adventure at every corner, your mind will wonder how the views seem to be more impressive after each turn. You are now experiencing the Magic of Sedona!

Anything Is Possible!

As you venture further into the canyon, the water creates incredible reflective views and then, you reach the end of the trail. This canyon caresses you as you find all that's left in front of you is water, then you will know it is time to turn back and watch how the views and photographic moments change with each adjustment from the sun.

Trail Head Maps:

West Fork (Call of the Canyon):

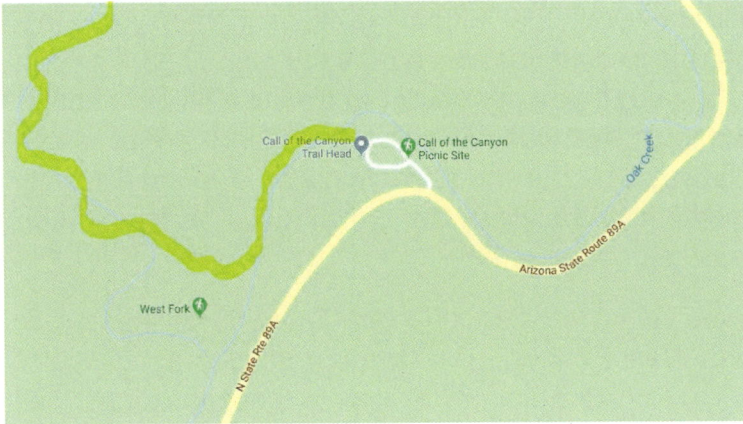

Distance (One Way):

West Fork: **3.3 Miles**

Elevation Gain: **Approximately 50ft**

Equipment Required:

- Some foot wear that you don't care about or some real good waterproof walkers or boots
- Walking sticks are ideal for people with stability issues or for avid stick users as crossing the creek can sometimes require assistance.
- Water is expected even though you are walking alongside a creek, you will need water
- Great cameras or really nice cell phone cameras. As usual, everywhere requires pictures
- Snacks are required as your journey may take you longer than you expected as there are countless pools to play in and stopping spots for you, your family and your pets!

Key Notes:

West Fork is ideal for summer hiking in Sedona as you will cool your feet along the hike. It is in your best interest to plan this one out as the lack of parking can deter you. If you don't want to wait in a line of cars for parking, you can find legal parking areas along highway 89A, but you better make sure you park legally and safely otherwise your car may not be there when you are done your hike.

If you've never hiked in Colorado or the Northeast US, then West Fork will give you a great idea as to what it is like to hike a flat creek area in those locations. Tall pines surrounding you with a mix of oaks and cottonwoods with colors from the rocks to the flowers. The cooler temperatures will also make you wonder why Sedona is even considered a desert and there is nothing more beautiful than hiking West Fork in the fall as foliage season is at its maximum! For me, it reminds me of my years growing up in Vermont, except I have Red Rocks instead of Green Mountains.

West Fork is a MUST DO for anyone that visits Sedona!

Elite Kid's Hike number 4:

Name: Cathedral Rock

Defined: One of the most photographed rock formations Sedona has to offer, this pair of monoliths with 'praying hands' in the middle has special shapes and ridiculous views from bottom to top. It is not an easy hike and is not for everyone as there is a 100ft seam to walk up that most folks will find too steep. But with proper guidance, it is well worth the exploration!

A Red Rock Parking Pass is required to hike here and for most of Sedona's hiking trails. Assume you need it when hiking any of these trails listed unless otherwise noted.

Trail Details: There are three entrances to Cathedral, but we will focus on the most direct route which happens to be the shortest distance. Entering from Back O' Beyond Road (located off Route 179, just 3.3 miles from the center of Uptown Sedona and 12.5 miles from Highway 17), it is a short windy narrow drive downhill to the parking lot area. Along this drive, you will be introduced to Cathedral Rock several times as it continues to get closer with each turn. You will notice the "Fingers" will be on the left side of your view of the rock.

Finding a parking spot might be hard, especially during Spring Break, but there are two parking areas; the first one is located .7 miles from the beginning of Back O' Beyond Road. The second parking lot is 50 feet further and on the same side of the road.

As you arrive to the trail head, you will see that the entrance to the trail is on the right side of the kiosk and

goes into a dry creek bed. During our monsoon season (approximately July to August), this bed can be filled with rushing water and not advisable to enter so be cautious. Once you cross the bed, you will begin the gradual ascent through the junipers with Cathedral straight ahead during your entire hike.

After several hundred feet, you will come to the 'ceremonial platform' which is where locals will celebrate weddings, anniversaries and even have drumming circles for full or new moons (which, in itself, is a tremendous energy sharing event here in Sedona), but they are not frequent occurrences. It just adds to the special energy that Sedona provides for everyone.

At the platform, you will also see trail connections to Templeton trail which circle Cathedral Rock giving folks on full day hikes, a double shot of wonder.

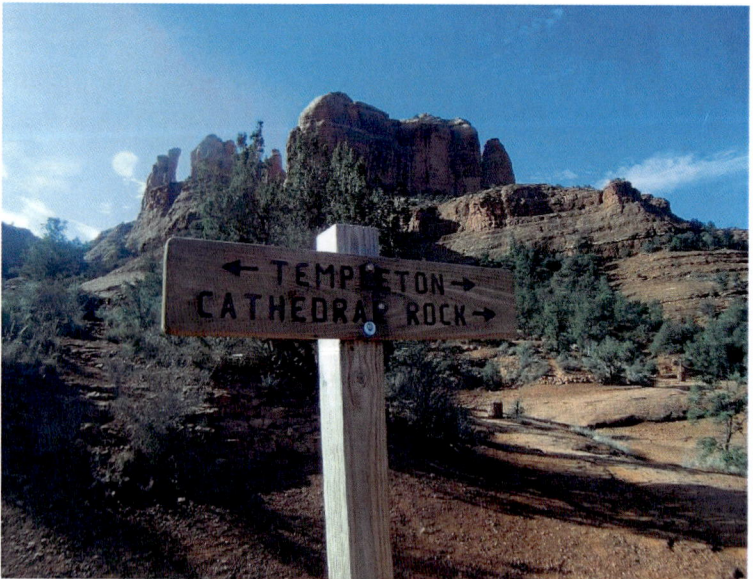

As you look around the platform, you will recognize the "cairns" (small baskets of rocks) distributed throughout the base area and the ascent. Simply follow these

The Seam

Cairns

towards the center-right as you look to the summit and they will guide you to the seam (mentioned before). There are several areas for your kids to play in prior to making the climb up the seam, feel free to explore to

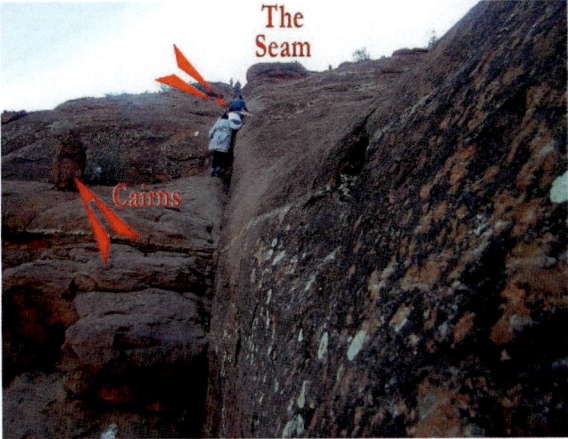

The Seam

Cairns

the left or right on those off-chute trails for added rock bouldering fun!

Now, to the seam climb! This seam is about 100 feet in length and is a tight, steep, step-by-step narrow pass that will bring you to the first shelf of views. About half way up the seam is a "Y" split that provides options to reach the shelf. Either way is equal in skill, so pick your poison here.

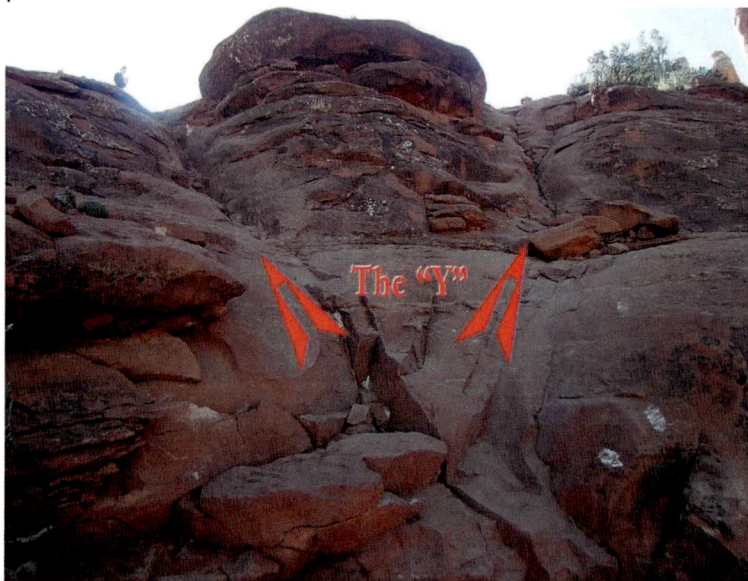

Understand fully that the seam is not to be taken lightly. Consider your options before you go any further. Older people and super young kids may not be ready, but you make the call.

Once atop the seam, the trail ventures up and to the right slightly. Again, follow the cairns to the easiest access. When you reach the second shelf, the trail will head left, but I want you to go right and follow the red rocks slightly around the corner for some incredible pictures of Sedona. If you position yourself properly, you will be able to capture pictures from as far west as

Bear Mountain and as far south as Bell Rock. Such an exquisite location for mega-photos!

Back on the trail, the ascent continues and fades slightly left. It will narrow through some trees and then open up gently to the 'saddle' of Cathedral. It is here that the grade begins to increase and the footing begins to decrease. There has been tons of foot traffic here so be careful for stepping on rocks that appear slick, as they most likely will be. Watch your footing as some rocks may be loose and can crumble or tumble under your feet.

There will be a few options in the last section as it seems to turn into a rock wall of sorts. You will see the trail steering you in a straight up direction, yet to the right will be some play areas for great picture moments. At the top, you will see the "END OF TRAIL sign

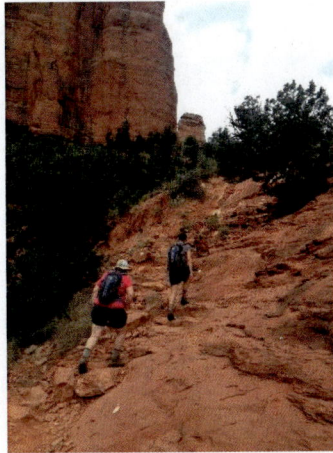

and it will be at the saddle. It is like a wall of stacked rocks perfectly placed for us humans to sit and relax or recover from the hike up.

You can bask in the glory of your accomplishments or you can venture to the right and sneak a fantastic and even jaw dropping picture on The Ledge! It's that corner off to your right that appears to have an endless

drop below. With the camera person at the trail sign and the 'posers' at the ledge, it will seem like they are at the edge of the world.

Your other option is to hike to the spires. The trail is left at the signage and it sneaks up into another saddle that is tighter and steeper with no real traction so you have to be cautious with your footing. When you find the top, it will have a couple of nooks to hide in and take in the energy of Cathedral. You can also traverse downward 50 feet or so and get up close and personal to the "Praying Hands" spires. These are those 'finger-like' spires of red rock that you saw on the top left of Cathedral as you viewed it from the parking lot. You can scamper around a bit to explore, but edges are all around. Be safe!

Trail Head Map:
Cathedral Rock:

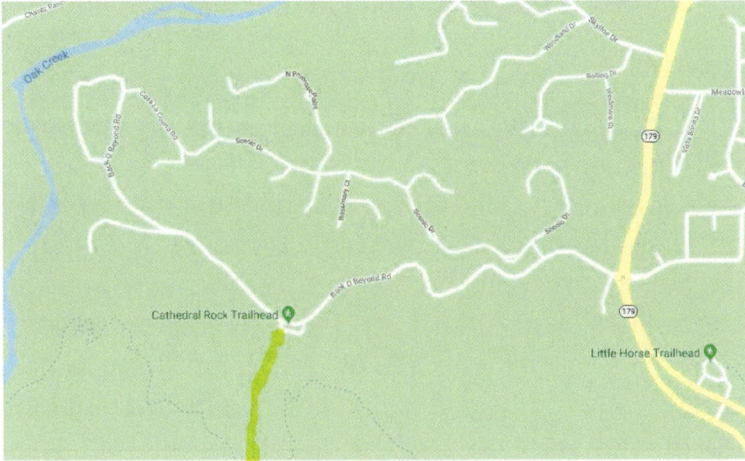

Distance (One Way):
Cathedral Rock: 0.6 Miles

Elevation Gain: **Approximately 750ft**

Equipment Required:

- Something with great traction. Rubber soles work best for the Red Rocks. Sneakers with synthetic rubber aren't as good as pure rubber soles, but they will do fine here.
- As always, water! Anywhere you hike in Sedona requires water. If you think you have enough, get a little more
- Great cameras or really nice cell phone cameras. Panoramic pics tend to show off Cathedral's views just a tad better than portrait or landscape style

- Snacks would be a good idea since you will no doubt remain at the saddle for some time relaxing and recovering from the hike.

Key Notes:

As mentioned previously, Cathedral is one of, if not *the* most photographed rock formation in Sedona. As you make your climb, you will clearly understand its beauty and the reasons why. However, I do need to mention that the seam described above is one to evaluate especially if you aren't an avid climber/boulderer. Some folks will tell you; "It's not much fun if you're not scared!". Well, I beg to differ and strongly disagree. You do not want to have a vacation end with you getting air-lifted or assisted by our Search and Rescue teams because you went beyond your skills. Make sure your Sedona adventures are safe and within your skills and desires. Keep it simple; if you are deciding if you want to go up, remember, it is always harder to come down.

For you avid climbers though, this will Rock your world with views! Your whole family will go bonkers for this climb and scampers, as well as the views. It just may be the hike that remains in your minds and hearts forever and your kids will always remember that you brought them there and conquered Cathedral Rock!

Elite Kid's Hike number 5:

Name: Devil's Bridge

Defined: With a name like Devil's Bridge, this is one of those hikes you have to put under your belt while visiting Sedona. A short one-way hike of just around 1.6 miles in length, it is a quick get, as the terrain is fairly level (as far as Sedona goes) with gobs of play areas along the way to keep the kids from getting board. It is a naturally formed Arch with a narrow pass-way at the top and a steep 100 foot drop off. It is not for those who fear heights or who cannot do steep stairs. There is one caveat for your hike; if you rent an ATV or Buggy or own a 4x4, you can cut 1.1 miles off this one-way distance as the actual trail to Devil's

Bridge is just about 1.1 miles from the Trail Head on Forest Road 152 (also called Dry Creek Road).

A Red Rock Parking Pass is required to hike here and for most of Sedona's hiking trails. Assume you need it when hiking any of these trails listed unless otherwise noted.

Trail Details: With only one access point (technically there are many more via other trail connections), this one is the easiest to find. The Trail Head Parking Lot is 2.2 miles from the intersection of 89A and Dry Creek Road following Dry Creek Road. You will need to be watching the road carefully as Forest Road **FR152** is fairly hidden on the right as you are taking a gentle left on Dry Creek Road. However,

you may have no problems finding it as there can be an overflow of cars parked on the sides of Dry Creek Road right around the FR152 connection.

Taking the right onto FR152, the parking lot is on your left within a few hundred yards. Park here if you do not

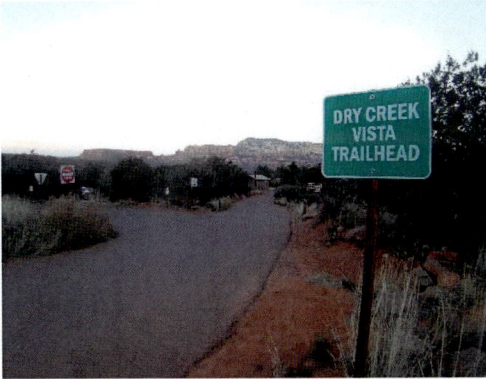

own a 4x4 vehicle as this road is very rugged and there are sign posts telling you that. If you do have access to a 4x4 (and we're not saying a Subaru-type vehicle is a 4x4, it is not, when it comes to this road), then your bumpy road ride begins here for about 1.1 miles until the Devil's Bridge Trail Head.

Assuming you are on foot from the trail head, you will walk the 1.1 miles northward and have a virtual party of pictures as both left and right sides will be filled with options for pictures. To your right, immediately out of your car will be Capitol Butte with a summit just over 6300 feet. At the far right on Capitol Butte is a rock formation we call Lizard Head. Some folks say it looks more like a dragon. As you continue to press on

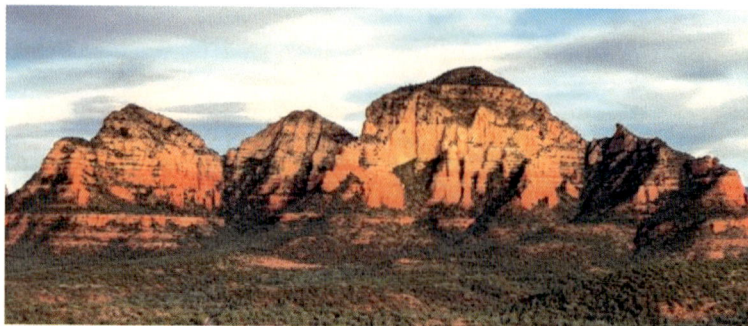

towards Devil's Bridge, you will see hundreds of caverns and seams boasting thrilling angles and shadows as the sun paints perfection all along the hike. You might get to see one of the hundreds of "Balancing Rocks" at the next outcropping on your right just after Thunder Mountain.

On your left and in front of you is what is known as the Secret Mountain Wilderness and it includes locations such as; Bear Mountain, Secret Mountain, Lost Mountain, Rattlesnake Mesa and a slew of other

catchy names for the formations in front of you. If you are hiking this trail during our monsoon season (usually July-August), you may find this trail a bit harder to walk through as the creek can be overflowing at times, so just check ahead for planning your hike.

The road has many turns and up and downs as you progress and on occasion, you will see some ATV or Buggies driving by. Give them plenty of room and watch out for dust. This walk can be a little extra hot

during the late May to late August as our temps will be in the upper 80's to 90's and it is wide open in the sun so try to bring long sleeves and a hat for sun protection. If you hike this during the fall and spring, the walk will be incredibly comfortable weather-wise.

When you arrive at the Devil's Bridge Trail Head, it will be on your right and kind of tucked into a pull-out but there will be a RED marker ensuring you are at the right

spot. There will be decent signage at the parking area and the trail is clearly marked. It will start you out scampering through some low pines and cypress and the canyon floor will slowly become surrounded by the canyon walls to the right and left as you follow along Devil's Creek and you will begin the steady ascent.

About three quarters of a mile in, you may catch a

glimpse of the Arch as you look forward near a large opening (just left of center in image at left). You will know it is the bridge because you will most likely see many people on the top of it. This just means your hike will start going up from here.

There will come a time where the trail will split off providing you a look from underneath the arch or the summit it. If you head to the summit, it starts to go

steeply up and will require hand and foot work for some people. Keep within your skills and desires and be safe. At the first bench (a lookout), you will be able to see the journey you just had as you can see out of the canyon, to Dry Creek

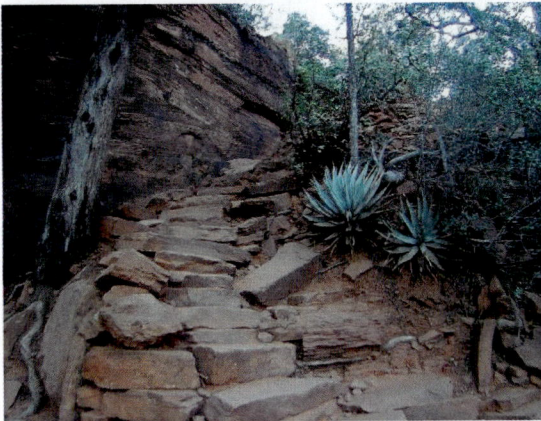

road and all the way across towards Secret Mountain. This is a great place to catch your breath.

You will then start climbing aggressively up and leftwards sneaking through some tight trees and shrubs. The stairs continue. You will reach a point where the trail steers to the left (Eastward) and it will appear that you have to hike down. It is merely an up and down to the platform for the arch. This platform is where most folks will stay for their final success and maybe eat and drink while absorbing more of the insane beauty.

You have the ability to cross the bridge from either the right side or left, however, the left side requires a jump of about four feet over a seam that drops about 50-100 feet straight down. If you are not up for that challenge, go to the right and follow the beaten path to the wide

end entrance. It will swoop up and around a few shrubs and then begin to descend as if you were heading down into the canyon again but it will veer off to the left and bring you to the arch itself. Many pictures are taken here as the arch is in the foreground and the entire canyon and walls of gorgeous red rocks are filling your backdrop.

Crossing the bridge takes some guts, but it has been safely traveled for many decades. Just stay in the middle of this narrow passage and make your way across, or don't. There is a nice meditation point on the other side worth the challenge. Just be SAFE!

Trail Head Maps:
Devil's Bridge:

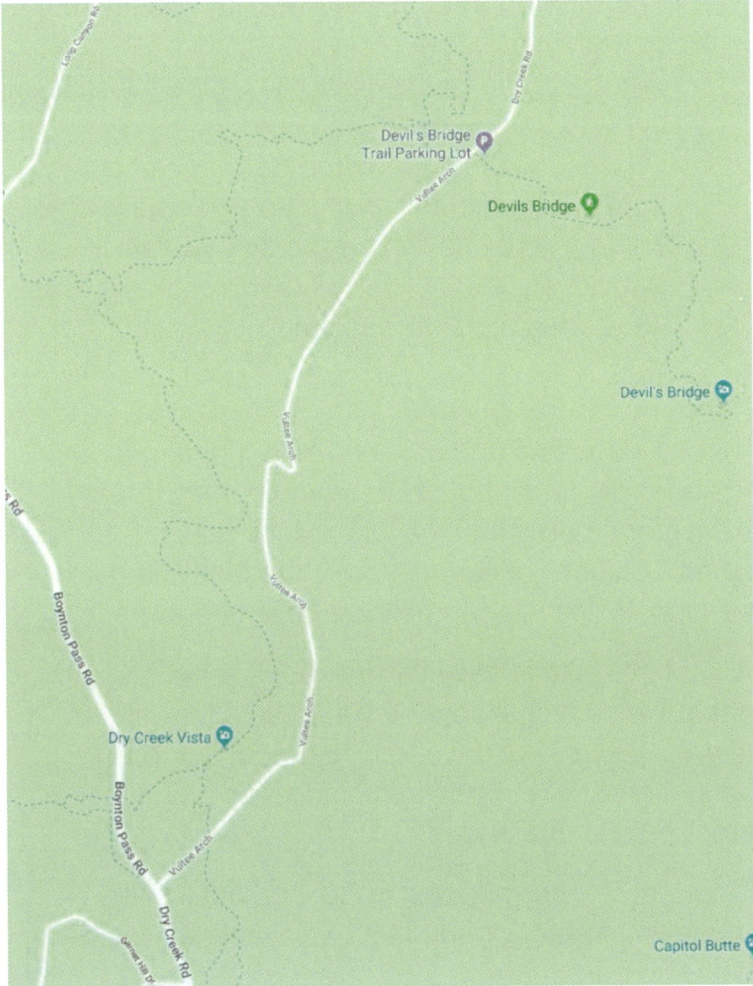

Distance (One Way):

Devi's Bridge Parking Lot: 1.6 Miles

Elevation Gain: Approximately 350ft

Equipment Required:

- Something with great traction and comfortable. The hike on the dirt road will have many rocks to walk over or on
- Water is critical especially if you take this hike in during our summer months
- Camera is almost required here as the pictures from the bridge are so unique and splendid you will regret not having a record of your visit
- Snacks are ideal especially since the walk in the wide open road will be long

Key Notes:

Devil's Bridge is a one of a kind hike moment for the entire family. It can be crowded so an early departure is best (and I do mean leaving around sunrise) to beat the foot traffic. Hot summer days are best hiked early morning or late day for the ease of temperatures.

90% of this hike is easy for anyone, it is the last 10% that makes it a challenge. If you have a fear of heights, you do not have to hike to the bridge as you can get great photography moments by going to the under-belly of the bridge.

There are 7 known arches in Sedona but Devil's Bridge is the easiest and most enjoyable as you will soon find out.

Elite Kid's Hike number 6:

Name: Scheurman Mountain Vista

Defined: One of the easiest and most rewarding short hikes you'll ever have in Sedona. At just around .8 miles in total length (one-way), this trail hugs the high school's solar panel lot and then streaks leftward and up a semi-switch-back ridge to the first bench. Then swings eastward (left) to the summit for the most complete scenic vistas Sedona has to offer, without the gobs of people around you!

*A Red Rock Parking Pass is required to hike here and for most of Sedona's hiking trails. Assume you need it when hiking any of these trails listed unless otherwise noted.

Trail Details:

Starting at the Sedona Highschool Administration parking area (see trail head map), this narrow path starts flat, and then begins a gradual incline about 300 yards in. The incline is a steady upward shift that is not hard at all, but the views will become incredible the higher you get.

After the Solar Panels, the trail turns to the left and passes an old gated fence allowing you to know you are on the right path. You will be slightly covered by junipers, pinyon pines and cypress for the next hundred yards or so as the uphill work begins.

Along the next ¼ mile, you will be seeing the wide open vistas of Sedona's West-end and right in the middle will be the giant Thunder Mountain (officially;

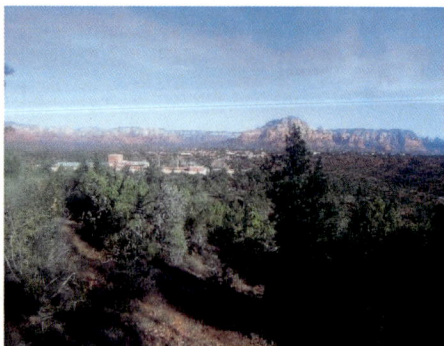

Capitol Butte) and to the right of it is Coffee Pot rock and even further right will be the big daddy of Sedona; Wilson Mountain. There will be no shortage of photo ops here and for the remainder of the hike.

There will be a stopping point around half way up to the first bench (mesa) that will have a couple large rocks

to sit on and enjoy the views. It is here that most folks choose to share sunsets as the entire Sedona gets lit up and you have one of the few spots that provides you with the entire Sedona view. Others will choose to scamper the remaining distance to the bench and then head left towards the signage that depicts the Scheurman Mountain Trail or the Scheurman Mountain Vista. The trail towards Scheurman Mountain Vista is our goal!

This portion of the trail is much easier and swings just to the right of the ridgeline. The prickly-pear cacti will be in bunches and the vast valley of Scheurman Mountain will come into view on your right. There will be pop-out mini-trails that will bring you to the top edge of the ridge facing Sedona and your options for pictures will be many. The trail

then skates gently upward until you enter the Fort Apache Layer of rock which makes the walking a tad rugged. Even though it is a mere hundred feet or so, one wrong step can end your easy hike so be careful.

When you get to the end of the trail, the views of Cathedral Rock, Courthouse Butte and even the Chapel of the Holy Cross will be fully in view. You will be getting a real clear image of how Sedona's "City" looks and how small it is compared to the monstrous Red Rocks. It is quite the impressive viewing area.

Trail Head Maps:

Scheurman Mountain Trail Parking Lot:

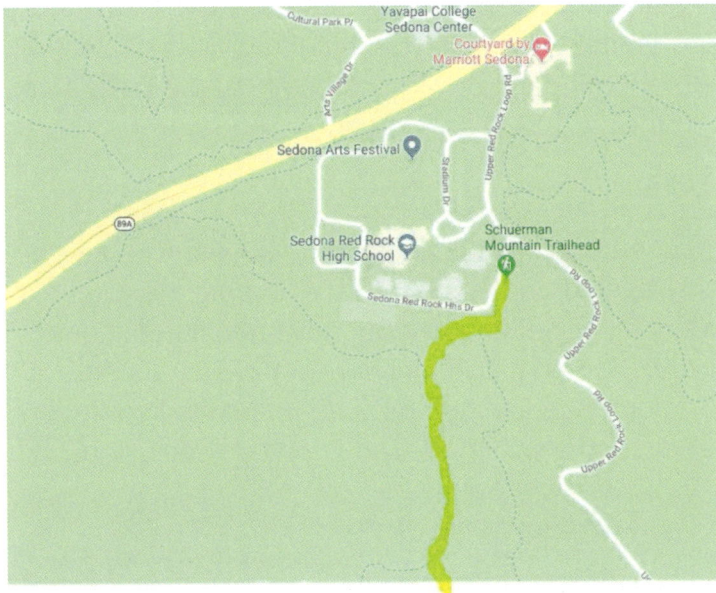

Distance (One Way):

Scheurman Mtn. Parking Lot: 0.8 Miles

Elevation Gain: Approximately 100-300ft

Equipment Required:

- Something with great traction is ideal but sneakers will be fine. Sandals can be ok, but you may want better ankle support especially at the end of the trail
- Water, water and more water. Even though this is a short trail, it is still in Sedona and Arizona and the sun is always ready to claim another victim of dehydration

- Great cameras or really nice cell phone cameras. Maybe a tripod or a good stand to help take vista pics and panoramas
- Snacks are always welcomed on a short trail and since you will most likely enjoy the vistas, they will be a great bonus

Key Notes:

Without a doubt, this is my favorite sunset hike as it is rarely traveled and easy to hike. It simply has the best views of all of Sedona without having to summit one of the BIG ones! It will not be as congested as the other more 'popular' sunset vista points and some great moments will be shared in private seclusion.

Elite Kid's Hike number 7:

Name: Sugarloaf Summit

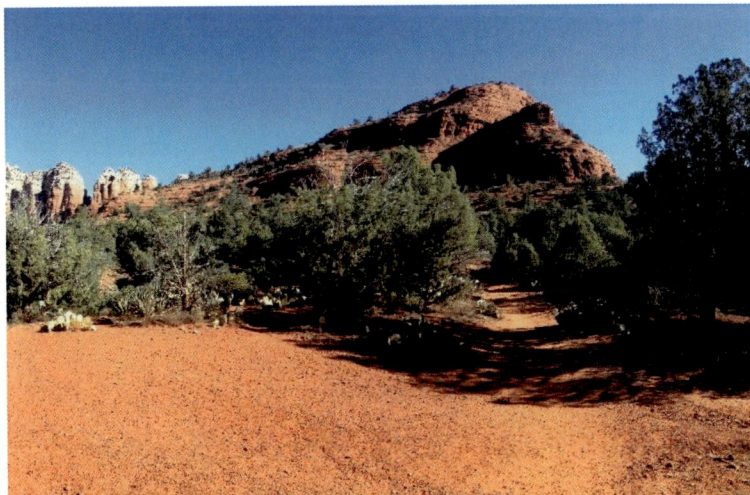

Defined: An incredibly simple hike and real easy with minor ups as you get to the summit trail portion. Sugarloaf Summit has this unique structure as it slopes upward at a roughly 25° angle for almost a quarter mile. The views are ideal for an early morning start or for an interesting way to see the City of Sedona at sunset!

*A Red Rock Parking Pass is required to hike here and for most of Sedona's hiking trails. Assume you need it when hiking any of these trails listed unless otherwise noted.

Trail Details: The Trail Head is off of Buena Vista Drive which is most easily accessed using Highway 89A to either Rodeo Road or Coffee Pot Road, then take Sanborn Drive and connect to Little Elf Drive (yes, we have a street with that name) which brings you directly to Buena Vista Drive and the trail head parking lot.

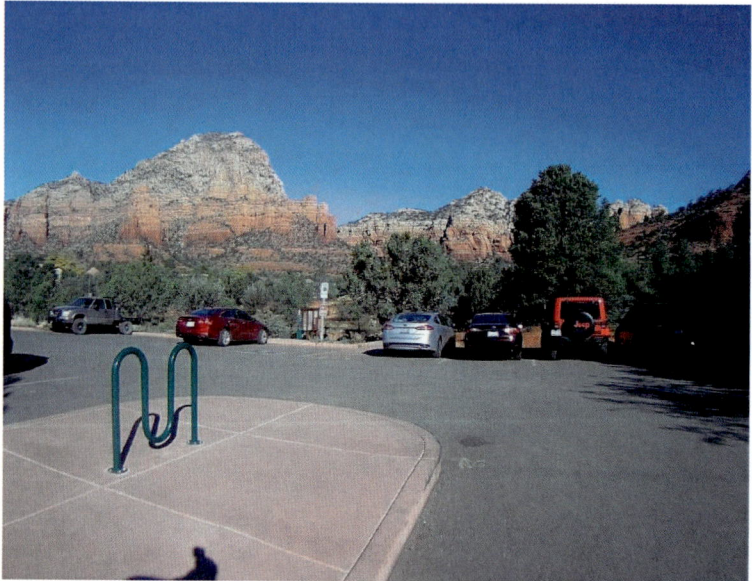

Once there, the trail you need is called Tea Cup/Sugarloaf and it is in the center of the image above next to the maroon car. This trail will lead you straight out towards the majestic Capitol Butte (also called; Thunder Mountain) which is also in the above photo and is the tallest summit in view.

This section is very easy and the entire hike can be done wearing any type of outdoor footwear including sandals. The trail is well marked and heavily trafficked at just around 0.3 miles. It will then merge with Thunder

Mountain Trail. At the junction, head right staying on Tea Cup/Sugarloaf. Around 100yards, you will meet the intersection for Sugarloaf Summit Loop Trail. Go

right for 100 feet or so and another intersection appears.

You will head leftward for another 100 yards or so until you find the signage for Sugarloaf Summit. This will begin a short switchback hike for about 0.2 miles all the way to the summit.

Your views will be a 360° introduction to where everyone lives in Sedona. Quite the spectacle and an even more impressive view once the sun sets!

*Interesting fact about the views from atop Sugarloaf; A large number of Western films were filmed in the area around Sugarloaf including one of the more famous movies; Angel and the Badman starring John Wayne.

Trail Head Maps:
Sugarloaf:

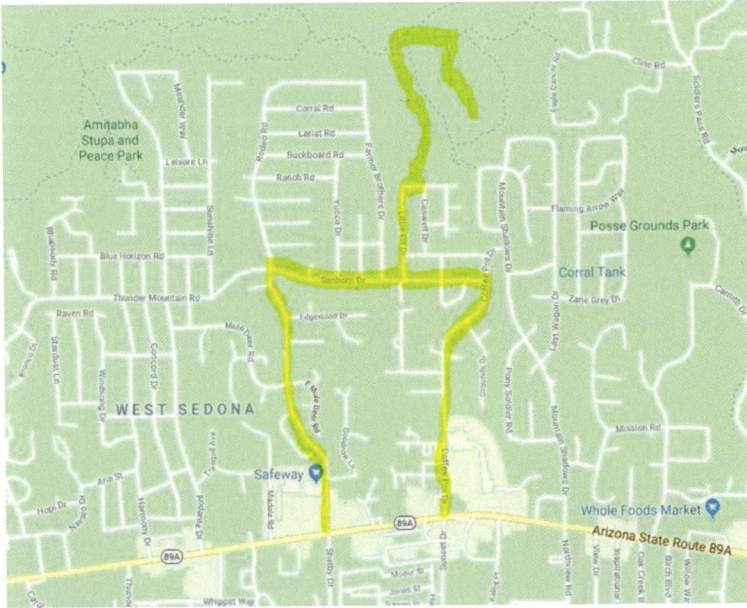

Distance (One Way):

Sugarloaf Parking Lot: **0.6 Miles**

Elevation Gain: **Approximately 350ft**

Equipment Required:

- Any type of outdoor footwear is fine. Some folks have done this barefoot, but I suggest something more than that. Sandals are fine as well
- Water is always suggested for any hike in Sedona. Don't ignore this one
- Great cameras or really nice cell phone cameras. A tripod may be ideal here if you have one and maybe gather some 360° images too.

- Snacks may not be needed here, but bring some anyway as you may want to venture off onto Tea Cup or Thunder Mountain trails after

Key Notes:

A wonderful simple hike for everyone and the views are more than worth the effort. The playtime that the kids will have will keep them smiling for days. Even the Big kids! Sunrise and sunsets are wonderful here so if you can plan one of those for this hike, it will really give you a dynamite bang for the buck!

Elite Kid's Hike number 8:

Name: Anaconda

Defined: A great scamper hike that will introduce you and your family to the central canyons of the Secret Mountain Wilderness which is essentially, the entire West side of Sedona's Red Rocks. There isn't any hard work here and it is perfect for any time of day. A distance of 1.7 miles from end-to-end, it is a perfect casual stroll on the knoll.

A Red Rock Parking Pass is required to hike here and for most of Sedona's hiking trails. Assume you need it when hiking any of these trails listed unless otherwise noted.

Trail Details: With the access to Anaconda being off alternate trails, I will give you the most common and easiest access available. The parking area is a mere 2.8 miles from 89A/Dry Creek Rd intersection and is a hidden left turn just before the Long Canyon/Boynton Pass Road "T". The pull off has been worn a bit, but may be fixed since this publication so be prepared for some pot holes and bumps on the 0.3 mile access road. Once at the opening, you will head to the far end straight ahead where you may see a small sign explaining you are about to head onto AZ Cypress Trail.

Park you vehicle as close as you want. The image above shows a vehicle parked about 100 feet away from the trail entrance.

From here, you will begin a creekside walk covered with Sycamore, Arizona Cypress and Juniper trees for just about one tenth of a mile to a trail split where AZ Cypress meets Snake. You are going to naturally take a left onto Snake, because what other trail would be more fitting to access Anaconda?

From here, you will be walking eastward through some ups and downs meandering through pockets of Red Rock and small hills and every so often, you will come across wonders of vistas showing off Capitol Butte, Bear Mountain and all of the Secret Mountain Wilderness range.

As you progress, you will begin a steady incline as you head around a knoll on your right (which is where Anaconda is). The trail has some small switch-backs to it and some quick ups but it stays relatively level. In approximately 0.5 miles, you will come across another intersection where Snake meets, Girdner and Anaconda. This is where you head onto Anaconda and begin a South-by-

99

Southwest journey climbing the knoll via some narrow switch-backs. It will be reasonably steep as you trek across the North face swooping Westward. Along that short climb, you will have gobs of stopping points to view the mountains, canyons and valleys around you.

Continue on and you will head back Eastward and flow along the top portion of the knoll. There are plenty of resting points and play areas for the kids but please make sure you walk carefully as the ecosystem needs to remain untouched as best as possible. As you caress the East ridge, you will be seeing Capitol Butte and the

canyon for Dry Creek along with Chimney Rock and other formations.

Now you will have the option of continuing on through Anaconda or turning around and heading back down. From start to finish, Anaconda is 1.7 miles, but if you choose to go down the back side of the knoll, you will add another 1 mile to get back to the parking area. It is well worth it however, as the views on the back side get you even more potential pictures of gorgeousness.

Assuming you have continued on, Anaconda will switch-back down the Westward side until it meets back up with AZ Cypress Trail. Make sure you head to the right for the shorter return because if you go left, it will take add 2 miles to your hike.

After a subtle flat hike of 0.2 miles, AZ Cypress will meet yet another trail called OK. However, you will not take that as you need to return on AZ Cypress to find the parking area. You will walk alongside the dry creek once again and depending on the time of year you visit, the creek could possibly be filled with water for some additional creative imagery. From here, it is 0.4 miles

until you reach the connection with Snake once again. Staying to the left at the intersection, there is a short 0.3 mile finishing hike to the parking area.

When all is said and done, you will have hiked about 3.6 miles and managed to see the farthest West

formation; Bear Mountain, all the way out to Lizard Head Rock and all points in between. Just magical!

Trail Head Map:

AZ Cypress to Anaconda:

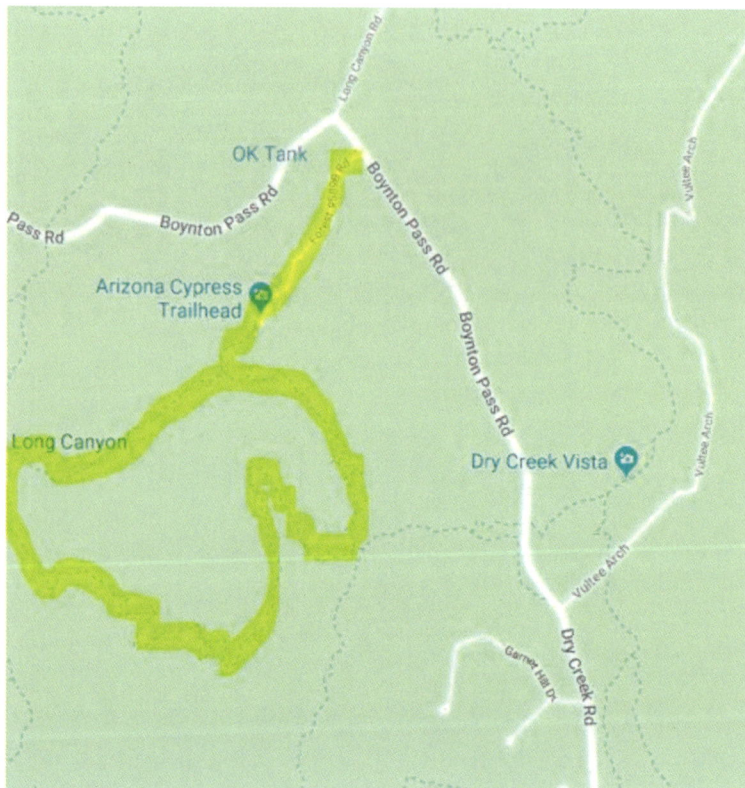

Distance (One Way):

Arizona Cypress Parking Lot: 3.6 Miles

Elevation Gain: Approximately 100-300ft

Equipment Required:

- Reasonable hiking shoes or sneakers, boots are always preferred for the additional ankle support

- Depending on the time of year, this trail can get pretty hot being largely in the wide open, so water is a MUST
- Great cameras or really nice cell phone cameras
- Snacks are ideal because there are gobs and gobs of stopping points for rest, relaxing, meditating and eating

Key Notes:

When I first found Anaconda, it was a mere child and very little wear and tear. Now, it has more wear and tear which means it is harder to lose sight of the trail. It is also one of my favorites for meditations and spiritual work as the silence is incredible and the views are amazingly wide open that you can actually feel the energy of Sedona while you stop and look around.

I like the subtle difficulty of Anaconda as it doesn't make it too easy to hike when ascending to the top of the knoll. You actually get to put some work into it to get to the real money shots.

Sometimes, I will simply hike up to the knoll top and walk around to the backside of the trail, but turn around and head back the way I came. That choice is all up to you. Just remember; keep it safe and take care of the land while you explore our vast trail system.

Made in the USA
Columbia, SC
06 March 2023